STEP INTO...
ANCIENT JAPAN

Fiona Macdonald

Consultant: Heidi Potter, Japanese Festival Society

LORENZ BOOKS

First published in 1999 by Lorenz Books

© Anness Publishing Limited 1999

Lorenz Books is an imprint of Anness
Publishing Limited, Hermes House,
88-89 Blackfriars Road,
London SE1 8HA

Published in the USA by Lorenz Books,
Anness Publishing Inc.,
27 West 20th Street,
New York, NY 10011; (800) 354-9657

This edition distributed in Canada by Raincoast Books,
8680 Cambie Street, Vancouver,
British Columbia, V6P 6M9

ISBN 1-85967-917-X

A CIP catalogue record for this book is available from the
British Library

Publisher: Joanna Lorenz
Managing Editor, Children's Books: Sue Grabham
Senior Editor: Nicole Pearson
Editor: Nicola Barber
Editorial reader: Richard McGinlay
Designer: Caroline Reeves
Illustration: Rob Ashby, Stuart Carter and Shane Marsh
Special Photography: John Freeman
Stylist: Thomasina Smith
Production Controller: Ann Childers
Picture Researcher: Adrian Bentley

Anness Publishing would like to thank the following children
for modelling for this book: Sarah Bone, Otis Harrington,
Rachel Herbert, Joshua Parris-Eugene, Levinia de Silva,
Nicky Stafford, Kirsty Wells, Tyrene Williams.

PICTURE CREDITS

b=bottom, t=top, c=center, l=left, r=right

Ancient Art and Architecture Collection: 17b, 19tl, 23br, 41tl, 42tl; E. Beintema/AAA
Collection: 22tl; Ronald Sheridan/ AAA Collection: 23bl, 35tl; AKG London: 1, 4br,
9br, 14tl, 35tl, 49tl, 50br; Heather Angel: 61bl; BBC Hulton: 29c; Bridgeman Art
Library, London: The Life and Pastimes of the Japanese Court 13tl; Sumo Wrestler
Abumatsu Rokunosuki by Kunisada 20tl, Fuji on a Fine Day by Kuniyoshi 23tl, Osen of
the Kagiya Serving Tea by Harunobu 25bl, The Moon by Kunisada 28, Woman by
Kikumaru 35bl, Standing Courtesan by Kaigetsudo 36br, Collecting Insects by
Harunobu 37tl, Salt Maidens by Harunobu 38tl, Threading a Needle by Chinnen 39tr,
Tales of Bunsho by Tosa 45tl, Tale of Genji by Tokugawa II 46br, Courtesan with
Musical Instrument by Kuniyoshi 48tl, Urban Life 49tr, Ships Returning to Harbour by
Gakutei 51tr, The Stone Bridge by Hiroshige III 51bl, Retreat in the Mountains by
Tomioka 51br, Woodblock by Yoshitaki 52tr, Yokohama Seascape 53br, View of Dutch
Trading Post 53tr, 53cl, Fuji in Fine Weather by Hokusai 55tl, Nicheren Calming the
Storm by Yoshimoro 56bl, Juroku Rakan 56tl, Cherry Blossoms at Asakura by Hiroshige
II 61tl; The following Bridgeman Art Library images are reproduced by kind permission
of the Fitzwilliam Museum, Cambridge: Mother Dressing Son by Harunobu 26tl,
Celebrated Beauties by Utamaro 36tl, Sudden Shower by Hiroshige 39br, Painting Party
by Kunisada 43cr, Fuji from Koshigaya 43cl, Mother and Baby Resting by Kunimaru
50tl; Christies Images: 3, 13bl, 16 bl & br, 17tl, 19bl, 23cl, 25br, 29bl, 35br, 37tr,
40br, 41tr, 44br, 53tr, 57cr & tl, 60tl, 60br; Bruce Coleman: 55bl; Asian Art and
Architecture Inc/ Corbis: 46tl, 47tl, Corbis-Bettman: 11tl, Carmen Redondo/ Corbis:
58br, Hulton-Deutsch/ Corbis: 21tr, Sakamoto Photo Research Laboratory/ Corbis: 28tl,
37bl, 47br, 57br, Seattle Art Museum/ Corbis: 21bl, Michael S Yamashita/ Corbis: 32bl;
CM Dixon: 10tl, 34tl, 45bl; Edimedia: 24bl, 26br, 38br; ET Archive: 4rl, 9rl, 11bl,
12bl, 20br, 27rl, 42br, 51tr, 52rl; Mary Evans: 2/bl, 34bl; Werner Forman: 10bl, 13cr,
15bl, 35cl, 39tl, 40tl, 49bc; Garden Picture Library: 57bl & bc; Michael Holford: 8br,
16rl, 18br, 22bl, 45br, 58tl, 61bl; Hutchison/Jon Burbank: 43tl, 54tl, 57cl; Hutchison/
JG Fuller: 54bc; Hutchison/ Patricio Goycoolea: 39bl; Hutchison/ Chiran Kyushu: 29cr,
39bl, Hutchison/ Michael Macintyre: 12tl, 31bl, br; The Idemitsu Museum of Arts:
19cl, 37tl, 41cl; Images Colour Library: 33tl, 57bl; Japan Archive:
2, 5tl & bl, 8tl, 9tc, 11tr & cr, 13tr, 14br, 15tl & tr, 17tr, 18tl, 20bl, 30bl, 31tr, 32tl,
33tl, 33bl, 43tl, 48br, 55tr, 59tr; NHPA: 61c, Tony Stone: 58bl; Superstock: 58bl.

Printed and bound in Singapore
10 9 8 7 6 5 4 3 2 1

CONTENTS

The Land of the Rising Sun............. 4

Eastern Islands..................................... 6

The Powerful and Famous.................... 8

God-like Emperors............................. 10

Nobles and Courtiers.......................... 12

Shoguns and Civil Wars................. 14

Samurai.................................... 16

The Way of the Warrior.............. 18

Peasant Farmers......................... 20

Treasures from the Sea................ 22

Meals and Manners...................... 24

Family Life 26

Houses and Homes.......................... 28

The City in the Clouds............................. 30

The Castle Builders.. 32

Towns and Trade....... 34

Palace Fashions.................. 36

Working Clothes 38

The Decorative Arts..................... 40

Wood and Paper.......................... 42

Writing and Drawing 44

Poems, Letters and Novels 46

At the Theater 48

Travel and Transport 50

Remote from the World............................... 52

Gods and Spirits.............................. 54

Monks and Priests 56

Temples and Gardens...... 58

Festivals and Ceremonies.. 60

Glossary.........................62

Index 64

The Land of the Rising Sun

IMAGINE YOU COULD TRAVEL BACK in time 32,000 years. That was when the first settlers reached Japan—a chain of islands between the Asian mainland and the vast Pacific Ocean. On their arrival, the early settlers would have encountered a varied and extreme landscape of rugged cliffs and spectacular volcanoes. Over the centuries, a distinctive Japanese civilization grew up, shaped by this dramatic environment. The Japanese people became experts at surviving in a harsh land. Emperors and shoguns, feuding samurai and peasant workers all played their part in the history of these islands. Many castles, temples, inventions and works of art have survived from the past to tell us what Japanese life was like in ancient times.

ANCIENT POTTERY
This decorated clay pot was made by Jomon craftworkers around 3000 B.C. The Jomon people were some of the earliest inhabitants of Japan. Jomon craftworkers were probably the first in the world to discover how to bake clay in fires to produce sturdy, long-lasting pots.

EARLY SETTLERS
The Ainu people live at the northern tip of Japan. They look unlike most other people in Japan, and speak a different language. Historians believe that they are probably descended from early settlers from Siberia.

TIMELINE 30,000 B.C.–A.D. 550

From around 30,000 B.C. onward the Japanese islands have been inhabited. For long periods during its history, Japan was isolated from the outside world. In 1854, that isolation came to an end.

*c.*30,000 B.C. The first inhabitants of Japan arrive, probably across a bridge of dry land from the continent of Asia.

*c.*20,000 B.C. Sea-levels rise and the Japanese islands are cut off from the rest of the world.

early pottery

*c.*10,000 B.C. The JOMON PERIOD begins. The Jomon people are hunter-gatherers who live mainly on the coasts. The world's first pottery is invented in Japan.

rice fields

*c.*3000–2000 B.C. People from the Jomon culture move inland. They begin to grow food crops.

*c.*2000–300 B.C. The Jomon people move back toward the coasts and develop new sea-fishing techniques.

*c.*300 B.C. The YAYOI PERIOD begins. Settlers from Southeast Asia and Korea arrive in Japan, bringing knowledge of paddy-field rice cultivation, metalwork and cloth-making techniques. Japanese society is transformed from wandering groups of hunters and gatherers. Communities of farmers live together in settled villages.

Yayoi bell

| 30,000 B.C. | 10,000 B.C. | 500 B.C. | A.D. 300 |

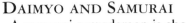

DAIMYO AND SAMURAI

A samurai swordsman is shown locked in mortal combat in this woodblock print. Daimyo (noble warlords) and samurai (highly trained warriors) played an important part in the history of Japan. Daimyo controlled large areas of Japan (domains) and served as regional governors. Samurai helped them keep control of their lands and fight rival warlords.

MAGNIFICENT CASTLES

During the 1500s and 1600s, Japanese craftworkers built many magnificent castles. This one at Matsumoto was completed in 1594–97. Originally, castles were built for defense, but later they became status symbols. They were signs of their owners' great power and wealth.

Sea of Okhotsk

CHINA
RUSSIA
HOKKAIDO
NORTH KOREA
Sea of Japan
JAPAN
SOUTH KOREA
HONSHU
N
SHIKOKU
KYUSHU
Pacific Ocean

THE ISLANDS OF JAPAN

The four main islands of Japan stretch across several climate zones, from the cold northeast to the semi-tropical southwest. In the past, each island had its own character. For example, northerners were said to be tough and patient, people from the central region were believed to value glory and honor more than money, and men from the south were regarded as the best fighters.

*c.*A.D. 300 KOFUN (Old Tomb) PERIOD begins. A new culture develops. New bronze- and iron-working techniques are invented. Several small kingdoms grow up in different regions of Japan. Rulers of these kingdoms build huge, mound-shaped tombs. There are wars between the kingdoms.

royal tomb

花刺蟲飛

Chinese writing

*c.*A.D. 400 The Chinese method of writing arrives in Japan. It is brought by Buddhist scholars and monks who come from China to work for the emperors of Japan.

*c.*A.D. 500 The YAMATO PERIOD begins. Kings from the Yamato region become powerful. They gradually take control of large areas of Japan by making alliances with local chiefs. The Yamato rulers also claim spiritual power, inherited from the sun goddess Amaterasu. Calling themselves emperors, they set up a powerful imperial court, appoint officials and award noble titles.

Mount Fuji

A.D. 400   A.D. 500   A.D. 550

Eastern Islands

JAPAN IS MADE UP of four main islands—Kyushu, Shikoku, Honshu and Hokkaido—plus almost 4,000 smaller islands around the coast. According to legend, these islands were formed when tears shed by a goddess dropped into the sea. The first settlers arrived on the Japanese islands about 30,000 B.C. By 10,000 B.C., a hunter-gatherer civilization, called Jomon, had developed there. At first, the Jomon people lived by the sea and survived by collecting shellfish and hunting animals. Later, they moved inland, where they cultivated garden plots. After 300 B.C., settlers arrived from Korea, introducing new skills such as rice-growing and iron-working. People began to live in rice-growing villages around A.D. 300. In time, groups of these villages came to be controlled by local lords.

Around A.D. 500, the rulers of Yamato in central Japan became stronger than the rulers of the other regions. They claimed the right to rule all of Japan and to be honored as emperors. These emperors built new cities, where they lived with their courtiers. However, by 1185, rule of the country had passed to shoguns (military rulers). There were bitter civil wars when rival warlords fought to become shogun. In 1603, the wars ended when the mighty Tokugawa Ieyasu became shogun. For over 250 years the shogun came from the Tokugawa family. They controlled Japan until 1868, when Emperor Meiji regained the emperor's ancient ruling power.

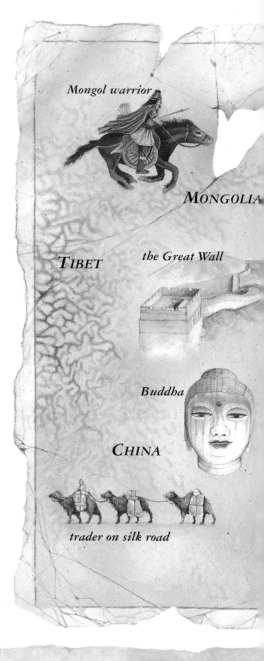

Mongol warrior

MONGOLIA

TIBET

the Great Wall

Buddha

CHINA

trader on silk road

TIMELINE A.D. 550–1200

A.D. 552 Buddhism arrives in Japan from China and Korea.

A.D. 585–587 Emperor Yomei decides to follow the Buddhist faith. Subsequent emperors also promote Buddhism.

A.D. 646 Emperor Kotoku makes new laws strengthening royal power.

Buddha

A.D. 701 Taiho Lawcode brings together many laws, setting up a new system of government. It is strongly influenced by Chinese ideas.

A.D. 710 The NARA PERIOD begins. A new government capital city *palace at Kyoto* is built at Nara.

A.D. 712–720 First historical chronicles of Japan, the *Kokiji* (Records of Ancient Matters) and *Nihon Shoki* (Chronicles of Japan) are completed.

A.D. 724–749 Reign of Emperor Shomu.

A.D. 794 End of the NARA PERIOD. The HEIAN PERIOD begins.

A.D. 794 Emperor Kammu moves to a new capital at Heian-kyo (modern Kyoto).

c.A.D. 800 The Fujiwara clan of nobles begin to control the government.

c.A.D. 800 Japanese culture replaces Chinese culture at the emperor's court. A new Japanese system of writing is invented.

Chinese vase

A.D. 550   A.D. 650   A.D. 750   A.D. 850

POWERFUL NEIGHBORS

Japan's nearest neighbors are China and Korea, two of the world's most advanced civilizations during the period A.D. 550–1185. From them, Japanese people learned many valuable skills, including writing and woodblock printing. However, because it was surrounded by water, Japan remained independent and developed a unique civilization of its own.

N
W
S
E

Ainu man

HOKKAIDO

CHINA

Yellow Sea

southern gate, Seoul

samurai warrior

Sea of Japan

KOREA

torrii

HONSHU

rice terraces

Rynkyn Islands

East China Sea

Dutch trading vessel

SHIKOKU

Mount Fuji

Pacific Ocean

Kong Fuzi (Confucius)

KYUSHU

to the Rynkyn Islands

A.D. 894 Links with China are broken.

c.A.D. 900 The invention of new scripts for written Japanese leads to the growth of various kinds of literature. These works include collections of poetry, diaries, notebooks and novels. Many of the finest examples are written by rich, well-educated women at the emperor's court.

c.A.D. 965 The birth of Sei Shonagon. Sei Shonagon is a courtier admired for her learning and for her witty and outspoken comments on people, places and events. She writes a famous pillow book (diary).

c.A.D. 1000 *The Tale of Genji*, written by Lady Murasaki Shikibu, is completed. This was a story of love, politics and intrigue within the royal court. *The Tale of Genji* is one of the world's first novels. Lady Murasaki was the daughter of a powerful nobleman. She began to write after the death of her husband.

Lady Murasaki

A.D. 1159 The Heiji civil war breaks out between two powerful clans, the Taira and the Minamoto. The Taira are victorious.

A.D. 1185 Successive emperors lose control of the regions to warlike nobles. The HEIAN PERIOD ends. The Minamoto family, led by Minamoto Yoritomo, defeat the Taira. They gain control of most of Japan and set up a rival government at Kamakura, far from Kyoto, the imperial city. Yoritomo takes the title of shogun.

Minamoto Yoritomo

A.D. 1000

A.D. 1100

A.D. 1200

The Powerful and Famous

THE HISTORY OF ANCIENT JAPAN records the deeds of famous heroes, powerful emperors and bold warriors. Men and women who had won respect for their achievements in learning, religion and the arts were also held in high regard. In early Japanese society, royal traditions, honor, skill and bravery in battle were considered to be very important, as was devotion to serious study. These principles mattered far more than the accumulation of wealth, or the invention of something new. During the Tokugawa period (1600–1868), many successful business people who were in the lowest social class gained financial power. Hardworking farmers, though respected, led very difficult lives.

PRINCE YAMATO
Many stories were told about the daring adventures of this legendary hero. Prince Yamato probably never existed, but he is important because he symbolizes the power of Japan's first emperors. These emperors came from the Yamato region.

EMPRESS JINGU (ruled c.A.D. 200)
According to Japanese legends, Empress (Kogo) Jingu ruled in about A.D. 200 on behalf of her son. Many legends tell of her magic skills, such as her ability to control the waves and tides.

TIMELINE A.D. 1200–1868

c.A.D. 1200 Trade increases and a new coinage is developed. Zen Buddhism becomes popular during this period, especially with samurai warriors.

A.D. 1274–1281 Mongols attempt to invade, but are driven back by storms.

samurai warrior

A.D. 1331–1333 Emperor Godaigo tries to win back royal power. He fails, but his bid leads to a rebellion against the shogun.

A.D. 1336 Ashikaga Takauji takes power and installs Emperor Komyo. He moves his court to Kyoto and encourages art and culture. Links with China are re-opened.

A.D. 1338 Ashikaga Takauji takes the title shogun. The MUROMACHI PERIOD begins.

A.D. 1467–1477 The Onin War— a civil war between rival nobles and provincial governors. The shogun's power collapses for *samurai swords* a while. This is the first in a series of civil wars lasting until the 1590s. New daimyo (warlords) conquer vast territories in different regions.

A.D. 1540 The first European traders and missionaries arrive in Japan. European traders hope to find spices and rich silks. European missionaries want to spread the Christian faith throughout Japan.

Portuguese sailor

A.D. 1200   A.D. 1300   A.D. 1400   A.D. 1500

LADY MURASAKI SHIKIBU (c. A.D. 978–1014)

The writer Lady Murasaki spent much of her life at the royal court as an attendant to Empress Akiko. Her book, *The Tale of Genji*, tells the story of the life and loves of Genji, a Japanese prince, in a sensitive and poetic style.

TOYOTOMI HIDEYOSHI (1536–1598)

Hideyoshi was a famous war-leader. Along with two other great warlords, Oda Nobunaga and Tokugawa Ieyasu, he helped unite Japan. The country was unified in 1590, after years of bloody civil war. As a peace measure, Hideyoshi banned everyone except samurai from carrying swords.

THE MEIJI EMPEROR (1852–1912)

The Meiji imperial family is shown in this painting. The emperor began his reign in 1867. The following year the shoguns' long period in office was ended when nobles (daimyo) engineered their downfall. The nobles then installed the emperor as a figurehead ruler.

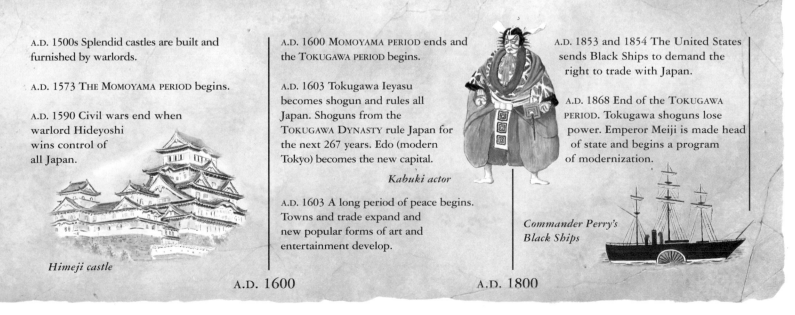

A.D. 1500s Splendid castles are built and furnished by warlords.

A.D. 1573 THE MOMOYAMA PERIOD begins.

A.D. 1590 Civil wars end when warlord Hideyoshi wins control of all Japan.

Himeji castle

A.D. 1600 MOMOYAMA PERIOD ends and the TOKUGAWA PERIOD begins.

A.D. 1603 Tokugawa Ieyasu becomes shogun and rules all Japan. Shoguns from the TOKUGAWA DYNASTY rule Japan for the next 267 years. Edo (modern Tokyo) becomes the new capital.

Kabuki actor

A.D. 1603 A long period of peace begins. Towns and trade expand and new popular forms of art and entertainment develop.

A.D. 1853 and 1854 The United States sends Black Ships to demand the right to trade with Japan.

A.D. 1868 End of the TOKUGAWA PERIOD. Tokugawa shoguns lose power. Emperor Meiji is made head of state and begins a program of modernization.

Commander Perry's Black Ships

A.D. 1600

A.D. 1800

God-like Emperors

HANIWA FIGURE
From around A.D. 500 to A.D. 550, hollow clay figures were placed around the edges of tombs. These figures, shaped like humans or animals, are known as Haniwa.

THE JAPANESE PEOPLE began to live in villages in about 300 B.C. Over the next 600 years, the richest and most powerful of these villages became the centers of small kingdoms, controlling the surrounding lands. By about A.D. 300, a kingdom based on the Yamato Plain in south-central Japan became bigger and stronger than the rest. It was ruled by chiefs of an *uji* (clan) who claimed to be descended from the sun goddess. The chiefs of this sun-clan were not only army commanders—they were priests, governors, law-makers and controllers of their people's treasure and food supply. Over the years, their powers increased. By around A.D. 500, sun-clan chiefs from Yamato ruled most of Japan. They claimed power as emperors and organized lesser chiefs to work for them, giving them noble titles as a reward. Each emperor chose his own successor from within the sun-clan and handed over to him the sacred symbols of imperial power— a jewel, a mirror and a sword. Sometimes, if a male successor to the throne was not old enough to rule, an empress would rule as regent in his place.

Descendants of these early emperors still rule Japan today. However, at times they had very little power. Some emperors played an active part in politics, but others spent their time shut away from the outside world. Today, the emperor has only a ceremonial role in the government of Japan.

NARA
This shrine is in the ancient city of Nara. Originally called Heijokyo, Nara was founded by Empress Gemmei (who ruled from A.D. 707 to 715) as a new capital for her court. The city was planned and built in Chinese style with streets arranged in a grid pattern. The Imperial Palace was situated at the northern edge.

FANTASTIC STORIES

Prince Shotoku (A.D. 574–622) was descended from the imperial family and from another powerful clan, the Soga. He never became emperor, but ruled as regent for 30 years on behalf of Empress Suiko. Many fantastic stories were told about him—for example, he was able to speak as soon as he was born. It was also said that he could see into the future. More accurate reports of his achievements list his introduction of a new calendar and his reform of government, based on Chinese ideas. He was also a supporter of the new Buddhist faith, introduced from China.

LARGEST WOODEN STRUCTURE

The Hall of the Great Buddha at Nara was founded on the orders of Emperor Shomu in A.D. 745. The whole temple complex is said to be the largest wooden structure in the world. It houses a bronze statue of the Buddha, 52 feet tall and weighing 500 tons, and was designed to display the emperor's wealth and power. There is a treasury close to the Hall of the Great Buddha, built in A.D. 756. This housed the belongings of Emperor Shomu and his wife, Empress Komyo. The treasury still contains many rare and valuable items.

BURIAL MOUNDS

The Yamato emperors were buried in huge, mound-shaped tombs surrounded by lakes. The largest, built for Emperor Nintoku, is 1,575 feet long. From above, the tombs have a keyhole-shaped layout. Inside, they contain many buried treasures.

THE SUN GODDESS

The sun goddess, Amaterasu Omikami, is shown emerging from the earth in this print. She was both honored and feared by Japanese farmers. One of the emperor's tasks was to act as a link between the goddess and his people, asking for her help on their behalf. The goddess's main shrine was at Ise, in central Japan. Some of its buildings were designed to look like grain stores— a reminder of the sun's power to cause a good or a bad harvest.

Nobles and Courtiers

I N EARLY JAPAN, everyone from the proudest chief to the poorest peasant owed loyalty to the emperor. However, many nobles ignored the emperor's orders—especially when they were safely out of reach of his court. There were plots and secret schemes, as rival nobles struggled to influence the emperor and to seize power for themselves.

Successive emperors passed laws to try to keep their nobles and courtiers under control. The most important new laws were introduced by Prince Shotoku (A.D. 574–622) and Prince Naka no Oe (A.D. 626–671). Prince Naka considered his laws so important that he gave them the name Taika (Great Change). The Taika laws created a strong central government, run by a Grand Council of State and a well-organized network of officials to oversee the 67 provinces.

BUGAKU
A Bugaku performer makes a slow, stately movement. Bugaku is an ancient form of dance that was popular at the emperor's court over 1,000 years ago. It is still performed there today.

POLITE BEHAVIOR
A group of ladies watches an archery contest from behind a screen at the edge of a firing range. The behavior of courtiers was governed by rigid etiquette. Noble ladies had to follow especially strict rules. It was bad-mannered for them to show their faces in public. Whenever men were present, the ladies crouched behind a low curtain or a screen or hid their faces behind their wide sleeves or their fans. To protect their faces when traveling, they concealed themselves behind curtains or sliding panels attached to their ox carts. They also often left one sleeve dangling outside.

THE SHELL GAME
You will need: fresh clams, water bowl, paintbrush, gold paint, white paint, black paint, red paint, green paint, water container.

1 Ask an adult to boil the clams. Let them cool and then remove the insides. Wash the shells and let them dry. When dry, paint the shells gold.

2 Carefully pull each pair of shells apart. Now paint an identical design on each of a pair of clam shells. Start by painting a white, round face.

3 Add features to the face. In the past, popular pictures, such as scenes from the *Tale of Genji*, were painted on the shell pairs.

NOBLES AT COURT
Two nobles are shown here riding a splendid horse. Noblemen at the imperial court spent much of their time on government business. They also practiced their riding and fighting skills, took part in court ceremonies, and read and wrote poetry.

THE FUJIWARA CLAN
Fujiwara Teika (1162–1241) was a poet and a member of the Fujiwara clan. This influential family gained power at court by arranging the marriages of their daughters to young princes and emperors. Between A.D. 724 and 1900, 54 of the 76 emperors of Japan had mothers who were related to the Fujiwara clan.

THE IMPERIAL COURT
Life at court was both elegant and refined. The buildings were exquisite and set in beautiful gardens. Paintings based on the writings of courtiers show some of the famous places they enjoyed visiting.

A LOOK INSIDE
This scroll painting shows rooms inside the emperor's palace and groups of courtiers strolling in the gardens outside. Indoors, the rooms are divided up by silken blinds, and the courtiers sit on mats and cushions.

4 Paint several pairs of clam shells with various designs. Make sure that each pair of shells has an identical picture. Let the painted shells dry.

5 Turn all your shells face down and mix them up well. Turn over one shell then challenge your opponent to pick the shell that matches yours.

6 If the two shells do not match, turn them over and try again. If they match, your opponent takes the shells. Take turns challenging each other.

The person with the most shells wins! Noble ladies at the imperial court enjoyed playing the shell game. This is a simplified version of the game they used to play.

Shoguns and Civil Wars

IN 1159, a bloody civil war, known as the Heiji War, broke out in Japan between two powerful clans, the Taira and the Minamoto. The Taira were victorious in the Heiji War, and they controlled the country's government for 26 years. However, the Minamoto rose again and regrouped to defeat the Taira in 1185.

Yoritomo, leader of the Minamoto clan, became the most powerful man in Japan and set up a new headquarters in the city of Kamakura. The emperor continued to act as head of the government in Kyoto, but he was effectively powerless.

For almost the next 700 years, until 1868, military commanders such as Yoritomo were the real rulers of Japan. They were known by the title *sei i tai shogun*, an army term meaning Great General Subduing the Barbarians.

SHOGUN FOR LIFE
Minamoto Yoritomo was the first to take the title shogun and to pass the title on to his sons. In fact, the title did not stay in the Minamoto family for long because the family line died out in 1219. But new shogun families soon took its place.

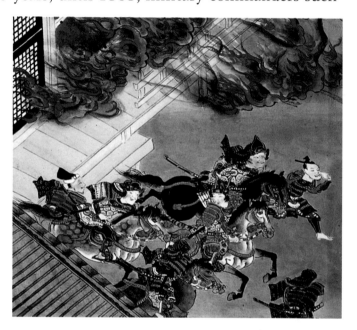

FIRE! FIRE!
This scroll-painting illustrates the end of a siege during the Heiji War. The war was fought between two powerful clans, the Taira and the Minamoto. The rival armies set fire to buildings by shooting burning arrows to drive the inhabitants out into the open where they could be killed.

MAKE A KITE
You will need: 23 x 33 in card stock, ruler, pencil, dowels tapered at each end (5 20 in sticks, 2 28 in sticks), masking tape, scissors, glue, brush, thread, paintbrush, paints, water container, paper (20 x 20 in), string, bamboo stick.

1 Draw a 20 x 20 in square on card stock with a line down the center. Lay the dowels on the square. Glue the sticks to each other and then tape.

2 When the glue has dried, remove the masking tape. Take the frame off the card stock. Bind the corners of the frame with the strong thread.

3 Now position your two longer dowels so that they cross in the middle of the square. Glue and then bind the corners with the strong thread.

DYNASTY FOUNDER

Tokugawa Ieyasu (1542-1616) was a noble from eastern Japan. He was one of three powerful warlords who brought long years of civil war to an end and unified Japan. In 1603, he won the battle of Sekigahara and became shogun. His family, the Tokugawa, ruled Japan for the next 267 years.

RESTING PLACE

This mausoleum (burial chamber) was built at Nikko in north-central Japan. It was created to house the body of the mighty shogun Tokugawa Ieyasu. Three times a year, Ieyasu's descendants traveled to Nikko to pay homage to their great ancestor.

UNDER ATTACK

Life in Nijo Castle, Kyoto, is shown in great detail on this painted screen. The castle belonged to the Tokugawa family of shoguns. Like emperors, great shoguns built themselves fine castles, which they used as centers of government or as fortresses in times of war. Nijo Castle was one of the finest buildings in Japan. It had "nightingale" floors that creaked loudly when an intruder stepped on them, raising the alarm. The noise sounded like a nightingale.

Kites were sometimes used for signaling during times of war. The Japanese have also enjoyed playing with kites for over 1,000 years.

4 Paint a colorful kite pattern on the paper. It is a good idea to tape the edges of the paper down so it does not move around or curl up.

5 Draw light pencil marks $1/2$ in in from the corners of the paper on all four sides. Carefully cut out the corners of the paper, as shown.

6 Glue the paper onto the kite frame. You will need to glue along the wooden frame and fold the paper over the edge of the frame. Let dry.

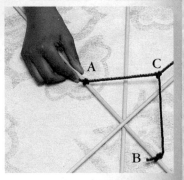

7 Tie a short length of string across the center of the kite frame (A to B). Knot a long kite string onto it as shown (C). Wind the string on the bamboo.

Samurai

Between 1185 and 1600 there were a great many wars as rival nobles (known as *daimyo*) fought to become shogun. Some emperors also tried, unsuccessfully, to restore imperial rule. During this troubled time in Japanese history, emperors, shoguns and daimyo all relied on armies of well-trained samurai (warriors) to fight their battles. The samurai were men from noble families, and they were skilled at fighting battles. Members of each samurai army were bound together by a solemn oath sworn to their lord. They stayed loyal from a sense of honor—and because their lord gave them rich rewards. The civil wars ended around 1600, when the Tokugawa dynasty of shoguns came to power. From this time onward, samurai spent less time fighting. Instead, they served their lords as officials and business managers.

RIDING OFF TO WAR
Painted in 1772, this samurai general is in full armor. A samurai's horse had to be fast, agile and strong enough to carry the full weight of the samurai, his armor and his weapons.

TACHI
Swords were a favorite weapon of the samurai. This long sword is called a *tachi*. It was made in the 1500s for ceremonial use by a samurai.

METAL HELMET
Samurai helmets like this one were made from curved metal panels, carefully attached, and decorated with elaborate patterns. The jutting peak protected the wearer's face, and the nape-guard covered the back of the neck. This helmet dates from around 1380.

SAMURAI HELMET

You will need: *thick card stock, pin, string, felt-tip pen, ruler, scissors, tape measure, newspaper, bowl, water, white glue, balloon, petroleum jelly, pencil, modeling clay, awl, paper, gold card stock, water container, glue brush, masking tape, paper fasteners, 2 8 in lengths of cord.*

1 Draw a circle with a 7 in diameter on card stock, using the pin, string and felt-tip pen. Using the same method, draw two larger circles 8 in and 20 in.

2 Draw a line across the center of the three circles using the ruler and felt-tip pen. Draw tabs in the middle semi-circle. Add two flaps as shown.

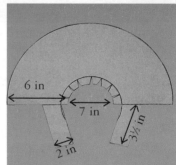

6 in
7 in
3½ in
2 in

3 Now cut out the neck protector piece completely, as shown above. Make sure you cut around the tabs and flaps exactly.

PROTECTIVE CLOTHING

This fine suit of samurai armor dates from the Tokugawa period (1600–1868). Armor gave the samurai life-saving protection in battle. High-ranking warriors wore suits of plate armor, made of iron panels, laced or riveted together, and combined with panels of chain mail or rawhide. Lower-ranking soldiers, called *ashigaru*, wore thinner, lightweight armor, made of small metal plates. A full suit of samurai armor could weigh up to 40 pounds.

SURCOAT FINERY

For festivals, ceremonies and parades samurai wore surcoats (long, loose tunics) over their armor. Surcoats were made from fine, glossy silks, dyed in rich colors. This example was made during the Tokugawa period (1600–1868). Surcoats were often decorated with family crests. These were originally used to identify soldiers in battle, but later became badges of high rank.

MAKING BOWS

Japanese craftworkers are busy at work making bows, around 1600. The bow was the Japanese warrior's most ancient weapon. Bows were made of wood and bamboo and fired many different kinds of arrow.

4 Draw the peak template piece on another piece of card stock. Follow the measurements shown in the picture. Cut out the peak template.

5 To make papier-mâché, tear the newspaper into small strips. Fill the bowl with 1 part white glue to 3 parts water. Add the newspaper strips.

6 Blow up the balloon to the size of your head. Cover with petroleum jelly. Build up three papier-mâché layers on the top and sides. Let dry between layers.

7 When dry, pop the balloon and trim. Ask a friend to make a mark on either side of your head. *Instructions for the helmet continue on the next page...*

17

The Way of the Warrior

SAMURAI were highly-trained warriors who dedicated their lives to fighting for their lords. However, being a samurai involved more than just fighting. The ideal samurai was supposed to follow a strict code of behavior, governing all aspects of his life. This code was called *bushido*—the way of the warrior. *Bushido* called for skill, self-discipline, bravery, loyalty, honor, honesty, obedience and, at times, self-sacrifice. It taught that it was nobler to die fighting than to run away and survive.

Many samurai warriors followed the religious teachings of Zen, a branch of the Buddhist faith. Zen was introduced to Japan by two monks, Eisai and Dogen, who went to China to study in the 1100s and 1200s and brought Zen practices back with them. Teachers of Zen encouraged their followers to meditate (to free the mind of all thoughts) in order to achieve enlightenment.

THE TAKEDA FAMILY
The famous *daimyo* (warlord) Takeda Shingen (1521–1573) fires an arrow using his powerful bow. The influential Takeda family owned estates in Kai province near the city of Edo and kept a large private army of samurai warriors. Takeda Shingen fought a series of wars with his near neighbor, Uesugi Kenshin. However, in 1581, the Takeda were defeated by the army of General Nobunaga.

SWORDSMEN
It took young samurai many years to master the skill of swordsmanship. They were trained by master swordsmen. The best swords, made of strong steel, were even given their own names.

8 Place modeling clay underneath the pencil marks. Make two holes—one above and one below each pencil mark—with an awl.

9 Fold a piece of letter-size paper and draw a horn shape on it, following the design shown above. Cut out this shape so that you have an identical pair of horns.

10 Take a piece of gold card stock Place your paper horns on the gold card stock and draw around them. Carefully cut the horns out of the card stock.

11 Paint the papier-mâché helmet brown. Next, paint a weave design on the neck protector, as shown. Let both items dry.

OFF TO WAR

A samurai warrior (on horseback) and foot soldiers set off for war. Samurai had to command and inspire confidence in others, so it was especially important for them to behave in a brave and honorable way.

MARTIAL ARTS

Several sports that people enjoy playing today have developed from samurai fighting skills. In aikido, players try to throw their opponent off balance and topple them to the ground. In kendo, players fight one another with long swords made of split bamboo. They score points by managing to touch their opponent's body, not by cutting or stabbing him!

kendo   aikido

SURVIVAL SKILLS

Samurai had to know how to survive in wild countryside. Each man carried emergency rations of dried rice. He also used his fighting skills to hunt wild animals for food.

ZEN

The Buddhist monk Rinzai is shown in this Japanese brush and ink scroll-painting. Rinzai was a famous teacher of Zen ideas. Many pupils, including samurai, traveled to his remote monastery in the mountains to study with him.

Samurai helmets were often decorated with crests made of lacquered wood or metal. These were mounted on the top of the helmet.

12 Bend back the tabs on the peak piece. Position it at the front of the helmet. Stick the tabs to the inside with glue. Hold in place with tape.

13 Now take the neck protector. Bend back the front flaps and the tabs. Glue the tabs to the helmet, as shown. Let the helmet dry.

14 Stick the horns to the front of the helmet. Use paper fasteners to secure, as shown. Decorate the ear flaps with paper fasteners.

15 Thread cord through one of the holes made in step 8. Tie a knot in the end. Thread the other end of the cord through the second hole. Repeat on the other side.

Peasant Farmers

Until the 1900s, most Japanese people lived in the countryside and made a living either by fishing or by farming small plots of land. Japanese farmers grew crops for three different reasons. They grew rice to sell to the samurai or to pay taxes. Barley, millet, wheat and vegetables were used for their own food.

Traditionally, Japanese society was divided into four main classes—samurai, peasant farmers, craftworkers and merchants. Samurai were the most highly respected. Farmers and craftworkers came next because they produced useful goods. Merchants were the lowest rank because they produced nothing themselves.

During the Tokugawa period (1600–1868), society began to change. Towns and cities grew bigger, small industries developed and trade increased. Farmers began to sell their crops to people who had no land of their own. For the first time, some farmers had money to spend on better clothes, houses and more food.

WRESTLERS
Sumo wrestling has long been a favorite sport in Japan. It developed from religious rituals and games held at farmers' festivals in the countryside. Sumo wrestlers are usually very heavy. They use their massive weight to knock their opponents off balance.

TERRACING
It was difficult to find enough flat land for growing crops in Japan, so terraces were cut like steps into the steep hillsides. Farmland could be shaken by earthquakes or ruined by floods. In years when the harvests failed, there was often famine.

RICE FARMING
Planting tiny rice seedlings in shallow, muddy water was tiring, back-breaking work. Rice farming was introduced to Japan soon after 300 B.C. Most varieties of rice can be grown in flooded fields called *tanbo* (paddy-fields). To provide extra food, farmers also reared fish in the *tanbo*.

FAVORITE FOODS

Soy beans and *daikon* (white radishes) were two popular Japanese foods. The Japanese developed storage methods that preserved them for months. The radishes were covered with earth, and the beans were dried, to provide essential winter food supplies. Farmers grew vegetables like these in small garden plots or in terraced fields.

daikon
radish

soy beans

A HARD LIFE

A woman farm-worker carries heavy baskets of grain on a wooden yoke. Although farmers were respected, their lives were often very hard. Until the late 1800s, they had to pay heavy taxes to the emperor or the local lord and were not free to leave their lord's land. They were also forbidden to wear silk clothes and drink tea or *sake* (rice wine).

THRESHING

Japanese farmers are busy threshing wheat in this photograph taken in the late 1800s. Although this picture is relatively recent, the method of threshing has changed little over the centuries. The workers at the right and the far left are separating the grains of wheat from the stalks by pulling them through wooden sieves. In the background, one worker carries a huge bundle of wheat stalks, while another stands ready with a rake and a winnowing fan. The fan was used to remove the chaff from the grain by tossing the grain in the air so that the wind blew the chaff away.

Treasures from the Sea

JAPAN IS A NATION OF ISLANDS, and few people live very far from the sea. From the earliest times, Japanese people relied on the sea for food. Farms, fishing villages and huts for drying fish and seaweed were all built along Japan's rugged coastline. Heaps of oyster shells and fish bones, thrown away by the Jomon people, have survived from over 10,000 years ago.

Japanese men and women took many different kinds of food from the sea. They found crabs, shrimps and limpets in shallow water by the shore or set sail in small boats to catch deep-sea varieties such as tuna, mackerel, shark, whale and squid. Japanese people also gathered seaweed (which contains important minerals) and other sea creatures such as jellyfish and sea slugs. Underwater, they found treasures such as pearls and coral, which were both highly prized. Specially trained divers, often women, risked their lives by holding their breath for long periods underwater to harvest these precious items. The sea also provided salt, which was collected in salt-pans (hollows built next to the sea). Salt was used to preserve fish and vegetables and to pickle many kinds of vegetables.

INSPIRATIONAL
Strange and beautiful sea creatures inspired Japanese painters and print makers to create many works of art. This painting shows two flat fish and a collection of shellfish. Tuna, sea bream and salmon were all popular fish caught around the coast of Japan. They were usually grilled or preserved by salting or drying.

DANGEROUS SEAS
Japanese sailors and their boat are tossed around by wind and waves in a rough sea. This scene is depicted in a woodblock print by Utagawa Kuniyoshi. The seas around Japan's rocky coasts are often wild and stormy. Being a fisherman was, and still is, a very risky job. Late summer is the most dangerous season to go fishing because monsoon winds from the Pacific Ocean cause very violent typhoon storms. These storms can easily sink a fishing boat.

SEAFOOD

Sea products have always been very important in Japan. Oysters were collected for their pearls and also for eating. Oyster stew is still a favorite dish in southern Japan. Mussels were cooked to make many tasty dishes. They flourish in the wild, but in Japan today they are also farmed. Seaweed was used to give flavor to foods. Today, it is also used as the wrapping for *maki sushi* (rolls of vinegared rice with fish and vegetable fillings).

oysters *seaweed*

mussel

FISHING METHODS

For many centuries, Japanese fishermen used only baited hooks and lines. This limited the number of fish they could catch on any one trip. But after 1600, they began to use nets for fishing, which allowed them to make bigger catches.

MOTHER-OF-PEARL

Made around 1500, this domed casket is decorated with mother-of-pearl, a beautiful material that forms the coating on the inside of an oyster shell. With great skill and patience, Japanese craftworkers cut out and shaped tiny pieces of mother-of-pearl. These pieces were used to decorate many valuable items.

OYSTER COLLECTING

Gangs of oyster gatherers collect shellfish from the sea bed. Both men and women are shown working together. Oysters have thick, heavy shells, so the workers have to be fit and strong to carry full buckets back to the shore.

GATHERING SHELLFISH

Painted in the 1800s, this picture makes shellfish-gathering look like a pleasant task. In fact, hands and feet soon became numb with cold, and the saltwater made them red and raw.

23

Meals and Manners

JAPANESE FOOD has always been simple but healthy. However, for many centuries famine was a constant fear, especially among the poor. The traditional Japanese diet was based on grains—rice, millet, wheat or barley—boiled, steamed or made into noodles. Many foods were flavored with soy sauce, made from crushed, fermented soybeans. Another nutritious soy product, *tofu* (beancurd), was made from soybeans softened and pulped in water. The pulp was formed into blocks and set aside to set. *Tofu* has a texture somewhere between custard and cheese, and a mild taste.

What people ate depended on who they were. Only the wealthy could afford rice, meat (usually poultry) or the finest fish. Poor families lived on what they could grow or catch for themselves.

Until the 1900s, people in Japan did not eat red meat or dairy products. But Japanese farmers grew many fruits, including pears, berries and oranges. One small, sweet orange is named after the Satsuma region in the warm southern lands of Japan.

FRESH VEGETABLES
A vegetable seller is shown here taking his produce to market. He carries it in big baskets hanging from a yoke supported on his shoulders. This photograph was taken around 1900, but the tradition of going to market every day to sell vegetables started some time around 1600. At this time many more people began to live in towns. The Japanese have always liked their food to be very fresh.

ONIGIRI—RICE BALLS

You will need: 7 cups Japanese rice, saucepan, wooden spoon, sieve, bowls, 1 tbsp salt, cutting board, 1 tbsp black sesame seeds, ¹/₂ sheet yaki nori seaweed (optional), knife, cucumber, serving dish.

1 Ask an adult to boil the rice. Sieve to drain, but do not rinse. The rice should remain gluey. Place, the rice in one bowl and the salt into another one.

2 Wet the palms of both hands with cold water. Next, put a finger into the bowl of salt and rub a little onto your palms.

3 Place one-eighth of the rice on one hand. Use both hands to shape the rice into a triangle. You should use firm but not heavy pressure.

SAKE

This *sake* bottle was made almost 600 years ago, in the Bizen pottery style. *Sake* is a sweet rice wine. It was drunk by wealthy noble families and by ordinary people on very special occasions. Traditionally, it was served warm from pottery flasks or bottles such as this one and poured into tiny cups.

CHOPSTICKS

Japanese people eat using chopsticks. Traditionally, chopsticks were made from bamboo, but today many different materials, including lacquered wood, are used.
In the past, rich nobles used silver chopsticks. This was mainly to display their wealth. However, they also believed the silver would help them detect any poison that had been slipped into their food. They thought that on contact with the poison, the silver would turn black.

ornate chopsticks

ordinary chopsticks

TEA

A servant offers a bowl of tea to a seated samurai. The Japanese believed that no matter how poor or humble people were, it was important to serve food in a gracious way. Good table manners were essential.

TABLEWARE

Food was served and eaten in pottery bowls and on plates. In contrast to the round and flat dishes found in many other countries, Japanese craftworkers often created tableware in elegant shapes, such as this six-sided dish.

4 Make more rice balls in the same way. Place each rice ball in one hand and sprinkle sesame seeds over the rice ball with the other.

5 If available, cut a strip of yaki nori seaweed into fourths and wrap some of your rice balls in it. To serve your *onigiri*, garnish them with sliced cucumber.

Rice was introduced to Japan in A.D. 100. It has remained the staple food of the islands ever since. Serve your Japanese meal on a pretty dish, and eat it with chopsticks.

The City in the Clouds

I**T WAS THE CUSTOM** for each Japanese ruler to build a new palace when he or she came to power. But in A.D. 710, the Empress Gemmei built a whole new city at Nara. It became the government center for all Japan. In A.D. 794, Emperor Kammu decided to build a city that would be bigger and even more beautiful than Nara. He moved his imperial court to a new site called Heian-kyo. Kammu based the plans for his new capital on the great Chinese city of Chang'an (present-day Xian). The whole city was laid out as a rectangle, with main streets running at right angles to each other. The emperor's palace was in the north of the city, and courtiers lived in elegant *shinden* (single-story villas) close by. Workers and lower officials lived on the outskirts. Heian-kyo (later called Kyoto) was home to Japanese emperors for over 1,000 years, until 1868 when Emperor Meiji came to power. Its royal and noble inhabitants became known as the people who lived in the clouds because they lived shut away from ordinary, everyday life.

IMPERIAL SHRINE

The Heian Shrine was built in 1895. It is a replica of the first Imperial Palace in Kyoto, which was designed for Emperor Kammu in A.D. 794. Like the original palace, it has red-painted beams and spectacular curving roofs in Chinese style. However, the shrine is just over half the size of the original palace. The shrine buildings stand in a garden, which surrounds a beautiful lake.

LIFE IN A *SHINDEN*

In Heian-kyo, nobles and courtiers lived in splendid shinden houses like this one. Each shinden was designed as a number of separate buildings, linked by covered walkways. It was usually set in a landscaped garden, with artificial hills, ornamental trees, bridges, pavilions and ponds. Sometimes a stream flowed through the garden—and through parts of the house, as well. The various members of the noble family, and their servants, lived in different parts of the *shinden*.

GOLDEN PAVILION

This is a replica of the famous Kinkakuji (Temple of the Golden Pavilion). The original was completed in 1397 and survived until 1950. But, like many of Kyoto's old wooden buildings, it was destroyed by fire. The walls of the pavilion are covered in gold leaf, giving out a golden glow that is reflected in the calm waters of a shallow lake.

SILVER TEMPLE

The Ginkakuji (Temple of the Silver Pavilion) in Kyoto was completed in 1483. Despite its name, it was never painted silver but left as natural wood.

THRONE ROOM

The Shishinden Enthronement Hall is within the palace compound in Kyoto. The emperor would have sat on the raised platform *(left)* while his courtiers bowed low before him. This palace was the main residence of all emperors from 1331 to 1868.

Towns and Trade

Until modern times (after around 1900) most Japanese people lived in the countryside. But after 1600, when Japan was at peace, castle-towns in particular grew rapidly. Towns and cities became great centers of craftwork and trade. As one visitor to Kyoto commented in 1691, "There is hardly a household... where there is not something made or sold." Trade also increased in small towns and villages, linking even the most remote districts into a countrywide network of buying and selling.

Castle-towns were carefully planned. Roads, gates, walls and water supplies were laid out in an orderly design. Areas of the town were set aside for different groups of people to live and work—nobles, daimyo and high-ranking samurai families, ordinary samurai, craftworkers, merchants and traders. Many towns became centers of entertainment with theaters, puppet plays, dancers, musicians and artists. Big cities also had "pleasure districts," where citizens could escape from the pressures of everyday life.

TOWN WOODWORKERS
Netsuke were toggles used to attach small items to a *kimono* belt. Three carpenters are carved on this ivory example. Woodworkers were kept busy in towns, building and repairing houses.

A TRADITIONAL TOWN
This picture was drawn by a visiting European artist in 1882. It shows a narrow, busy street in a Japanese city. Although it is a relatively recent picture, it shows styles of clothes, stores and houses that had existed for several hundred years. The buildings are made of wood, and the stores open directly onto the streets. The cloth hangings above the doorways represent the type of store—for example, a knife or fan store. They are printed or woven with *kanji* characters or special designs. The European artist obviously could not read Japanese because the writing on the store boards and banners is meaningless squiggles.

SKILLED AT WEAVING SILK

Silk was woven on a loom like the one shown here. This woodblock print dates from about 1770. Towns were great centers of cloth production. Kyoto, in particular, was famous for its silk fabrics patterned with gold and silver flowers.

MANY DIFFERENT CRAFTS

These two men are busy making paper lanterns. From the earliest times, craftworkers with many different skills worked in Japanese towns. One list of craft guilds, drawn up in Osaka in 1784, included 24 trades. They ranged from makers of porcelain, parasols and face-powder, to basket-weavers, printers, paper-sellers, paint-mixers, cotton-spinners, ivory carvers and makers of socks.

PLEASURE PURSUIT

Actors, musicians and entertainers, like this well-dressed young woman, lived and worked in the "pleasure districts" of many towns. The most famous was the Yoshiwara district of Edo. In big cities, they were full of inns and restaurants. Young female entertainers were called *geisha*. Merchants and sometimes samurai would enjoy a meal and a drink while the *geisha* danced and sang for their pleasure.

FIRE HAZARD

Fire was a constant danger in Japanese cities. This was because most buildings were made of wood and packed close together. In an effort to prevent fires from spreading, city rulers gave orders that wooden roof-coverings should be replaced by fireproof clay tiles. They also decreed that tubs of water should be placed in city streets and watchtowers built to give advance warning of fire.

Palace Fashions

IN ANCIENT JAPAN, rich noblemen and women at the emperor's court wore very different clothes from ordinary peasant farmers. From around A.D. 600 to 1500, Japanese court fashions were based on traditional Chinese styles. Both men and women wore long, flowing robes made of many layers of fine, glossy silk held in place by a sash or cords. Men also wore wide trousers underneath. Women kept their hair loose and long, while men tied their hair into topknots and wore tall black hats. Elegance and refinement were the aims of this style.

After about 1500, wealthy samurai families began to choose new styles. Men and women wore *kimonos*—long, loose robes. *Kimonos* also became popular among wealthy artists, actors and craftworkers. The shoguns passed laws to try to stop ordinary people from wearing elaborate *kimonos*, but they proved to be impossible to enforce.

PARASOL
Women protected their delicate complexions with sunshades made of oiled paper. The fashion was for pale skin, often heavily powdered, with dark, soft eyebrows.

GOOD TASTE OR GAUDY?
This woman's outfit dates from the 1700s. Though striking, it would probably have been considered too bold to be in the most refined taste. Men and women took great care in choosing garments that blended well together.

MAKE A FAN
You will need: thick card stock (11 x 10 in), pencil, ruler, compass, protractor, felt-tip pen (blue), paper (red), scissors, paints, paintbrush, water container, glue stick.

1 Draw a line down the center of the piece of card stock. Place your compass two-thirds of the way up the line. Draw a circle 9 in in diameter.

2 Add squared-off edges at the top of the circle, as shown. Now draw your handle (6 in long). The handle should be directly over the vertical line.

3 Place a protractor at the top of the handle and draw a semicircle around it. Now mark lines every 2½ degrees. Draw pencil lines through these marks.

FEET OFF THE GROUND

To catch insects in a garden by lamplight these women are wearing *geta* (clogs). *Geta* were designed to protect the wearer's feet from mud and rain by raising them about 2–3 inches above the ground. They were worn outdoors.

SILK *KIMONO*

This beautiful silk *kimono* was made in about 1600. Women wore a wide silk sash called an *obi* on top of their *kimonos*. Men fastened their *kimonos* with a narrow sash.

PAPER FAN

Folding fans, made of pleated paper, were a Japanese invention. They were carried by both men and women. This one is painted with gold leaf and chrysanthemum flowers.

BEAUTIFUL HAIR

Traditional palace fashions for men and women are shown in this scene from the imperial palace. The women have long, flowing hair that reaches to their waists—a sign of great beauty in early Japan.

It was the custom for Japanese noblewomen to hide their faces in court. They used decorated fans such as this one as a screen. Fans were also used to help people keep cool on hot, humid summer days.

4 Draw a blue line ¹/₂ in to the left of each line you have drawn. Then draw a blue line ¹/₈ in to the right of this line. Add a squiggle between sections.

5 Cut out your card stock fan. Now use this as a template. Draw around the fan top (not handle) on your red paper. Cut out the red paper.

6 Now cut out the in-between sections on your card stock fan (those marked with a squiggle). Paint the fan brown on both sides. Let dry.

7 Paint the red paper with white flowers and let dry. Paste glue on one side of the card stock fan. Stick the undecorated side of the red paper to the fan.

Working Clothes

ORDINARY PEOPLE IN JAPAN could not afford the rich, silk robes worn by emperors, nobles and samurai families. Instead, they wore plain, simple clothes that gave them freedom to move easily as they went about their daily tasks. Men wore baggy jackets and loose trousers, while women wore simple, long wrap-over robes.

Ordinary clothes were made from rough, inexpensive fibers, woven at home or purchased in towns. Cotton, hemp and ramie (a plant much like flax) were all popular. Many other plants were also used to make cloth, including plantains and the bark of the mulberry tree. From around 1600, clothes were dyed with indigo (a blue dye) and sometimes woven in complicated *ikat* patterns.

Japan's climate varies from cold and snowy in winter to hot and steamy in summer, so working peoples' clothes had to be adaptable. Usually people added or removed layers of clothing depending on the season. To cope with the rainy summers, they made waterproof clothes from straw. In winter, they wore padded or quilted jackets.

PROTECTIVE APRONS
These women are making salt from ocean water. They are wearing aprons made out of leather or heavy canvas cloth to protect their clothes. The woman on the right has tied back her long hair with a scarf.

LOOSE AND COMFY
Farmworkers are shown hard at work planting rice seedlings in a flooded paddy-field. They are wearing loose, comfortable clothes—short jackets, baggy trousers tied at the knee and ankle, and hats for shade. For working in water, in rice-fields or by the shore, ordinary men and women often went barefoot.

MAKE DO AND MEND

Working clothes often got frayed or torn, and it was a woman's job to mend them with needle and thread. Women in poor, ordinary families usually made rough, simple clothes for their own families. Sometimes they also bought clothes from traveling peddlers or at small stores.

ARMORERS AT WORK

Loose, flowing *kimonos* were originally worn only by high-ranking families. Before long other wealthy and prestigious people, such as these skilled armor makers, copied them. *Kimonos* were elegant and comfortable. However, they were certainly not suitable for active outdoor work.

FITTING FOOTWEAR

Outdoors, ordinary people wore clogs or simple sandals. The sandals were woven from straw and held on with twisted straw strings. Before entering a house, people always took off their outdoor footwear so as not to bring mud, grass and dirt inside.

KEEPING THE RAIN OUT

Cone-shaped hats made of woven straw or bamboo protected people's heads from rain. The sloping shape of these hats helped the rainwater run off before it had time to soak in. Farmworkers also made rain-capes out of straw matting. In this picture you can see one man bent almost double under his rain-cape (*right*). To protect themselves from the rain, rich people used umbrellas made of oiled cloth.

The Decorative Arts

THERE IS A LONG TRADITION among Japanese craftworkers of making everyday things as beautiful as possible. Craftworkers also created exquisite items for the wealthiest and most knowledgeable collectors. They used a wide variety of materials—pottery, metal, lacquer, cloth, paper and bamboo. Pottery ranged from plain, simple earthenware to delicate porcelain, painted with brightly colored glazes. Japanese metalworkers produced alloys (mixtures of metals) that were unknown elsewhere in the ancient world. Cloth was woven from many fibers in elaborate designs. Bamboo and other plants from the grass family were woven into elegant *tatami* mats (floor mats) and containers of all different shapes and sizes. Japanese craftworkers also made beautifully decorated *inro* (little boxes, used like purses) which dangled from men's *kimono* sashes.

SHINY LACQUER
This samurai helmet was made for ceremonial use. It is covered in lacquer (varnish) and decorated with a diving dolphin. Producing shiny lacquerware was a slow process. An object was covered with many thin layers of lacquer. Each layer was allowed to dry, then polished, before more lacquer was applied. The lacquer could then be carved.

SAMURAI SURCOAT
Even the simplest garments were beautifully crafted. This surcoat (loose, sleeveless tunic) was made for a member of the noble Mori family, probably around 1800. Surcoats were worn by samurai on top of their armor.

MAKE A NETSUKE FOX

You will need: paper, pencil, ruler, self-drying clay, balsa wood, modeling tool, fine sandpaper, acrylic paint, paintbrush, water container, darning needle, cord, small box (for an inro), scissors, toggle, wide belt.

1 Draw a square 2 x 2 in on a piece of paper. Roll out a ball of clay to the size of the square. Shape the clay so that it comes to a point at one end.

2 Turn your clay over. Lay a stick of balsa approximately 2 1/2 in long along the back. Stick a thin sausage of clay over the stick. Press to secure.

3 Turn the clay over. Cut out two triangles of clay. Join them to the head using the tool. Make indentations to shape them into a fox's ears.

METALWORK

Craftworkers polish the sharp swords and knives they have made. It took many years of training to become a metalworker. Japanese craftsmen were famous for their fine skills at smelting and handling metals.

BOXES FOR BELTS

Inro were originally designed for storing medicines. The first *inro* were plain and simple, but after about 1700 they were often decorated with exquisite designs. These *inro* have been lacquered (coated with a shiny substance made from the sap of the lacquer tree). Inside, they contain several compartments stacked on top of each other.

MASTERWORK

This jar is decorated with a design of white flowers, painted over a shiny red and black glaze. It was painted by the master-craftsman Ogata Kenzan, who lived from 1663 to 1743.

Wear your inro *dangling from your belt. In ancient Japan,* inro *were usually worn by men. They were held in place with carved toggles called* netsuke.

4 Use the handle of your modeling tool to make your fox's mouth. Carve eyes, nostrils, teeth and a frown line. Use the top of a pencil to make eye holes.

5 Let dry. Gently sand the *netsuke* and remove the balsa wood stick. Paint it with several layers of acrylic paint. Set aside in a warm place to dry.

6 Thread the cord through the four corners of a small box with a darning needle. Then thread the cord through a toggle and the *netsuke*.

7 Put a wide belt around your waist. Thread the *netsuke* under the belt. It should rest on the top of it. The *inro* (box) should hang down, as shown.

Wood and Paper

IN ANCIENT JAPAN, woodworking was an art as well as a craft. Most large Japanese buildings, such as temples and palaces, were decorated with elaborately carved, painted and gilded wooden roofs. Doorways and pillars were also painted or carved. Inside, ceiling-beams and supporting pillars were made from strong tree trunks, floors were laid with polished wooden strips and sliding screens had finely made wooden frames. A display of woodworking skill in a building demonstrated the owner's wealth and power. However, some smaller wooden buildings were left deliberately plain, allowing the quality of the materials and craftsmanship, and the elegance of the design, to speak for themselves.

Paper was another very important Japanese craft. It was used to make many fine objects—from wall-screens to lanterns, sunshades and even clothes. The choice of the best paper for writing a poem or painting a picture was part of an artist's task. Fine paper also showed off a letter-writer's elegance and good taste.

WOODEN STATUES
This statue portrays a Buddhist god. It was carved between A.D. 800 and 900. Many Japanese temples contain carvings and statues made from wood.

SCREENS WITH SCENES
Screens were movable works of art. This example, made in the 1700s, portrays a scene from Japanese history. It shows Portuguese merchants and missionaries listening to Japanese musicians.

ORIGAMI BOX

You will need: a square of origami paper (6 x 6 in), clean and even folding surface.

1 Place your paper on a flat surface. Fold it horizontally across the center. Next, fold it vertically across the center and unfold.

2 Carefully fold each corner to the center point as shown. Unfold each corner crease before starting to make the next one.

3 Using the creases, fold all the corners back into the center. Now fold each side ³/₄ in from the edge to make a crease and then unfold.

GRAND PILLARS

This row of red wooden pillars supports a heavy, ornate roof. It is part of the Meiji Shrine in Tokyo. Red (or cinnabar) was the traditional Japanese color for shrines and royal palaces.

HOLY LIGHTS

Lamps made of pleated paper were often hung outside Shinto shrines. They were painted with the names of people who had donated money to the shrines.

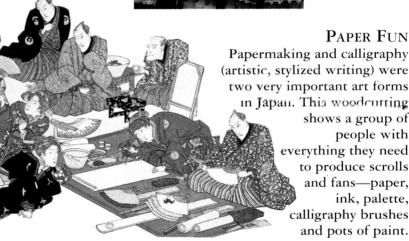

PAPER FUN

Papermaking and calligraphy (artistic, stylized writing) were two very important art forms in Japan. This woodcutting shows a group of people with everything they need to produce scrolls and fans—paper, ink, palette, calligraphy brushes and pots of paint.

USEFUL AND BEAUTIFUL

Trees were admired for their beauty as well as their usefulness. These spring trees were portrayed by the famous Japanese woodblock printer, Hiroshige.

Japanese people used boxes of all shapes and sizes to store their possessions. What will you keep in your box?

4 Carefully unfold two opposite side panels. Your origami box should now look like the structure shown in the picture above.

5 Following the crease marks you have already made, turn in the side panels to make walls, as shown in the picture. Turn the origami around 90°.

6 Use your fingers to push the corners of the third side in, as shown. Use the existing crease lines as a guide. Raise the box slightly and fold the wall over.

7 Next, carefully repeat step 6 to construct the final wall. You could try making another origami box to perfect your technique.

43

printed kanji	katakana	printed kanji	handwritten kanji	hiragana
阿 →	ア	以 →	い →	い
伊 →	イ	呂 →	ろ →	ろ
宇 →	ウ	波 →	は →	は
江 →	エ	仁 →	に →	に
於 →	オ	保 →	ほ →	ほ

JAPANESE WRITING

Around A.D. 800, two new writing systems, *hiragana* and *katakana*, were invented. For the first time, people could write Japanese exactly as they spoke it. The left-hand side of the chart above shows how a selection of *katakana* symbols developed from the original *kanji*. The right-hand side of the chart shows how *hiragana* symbols evolved, via the handwritten form of *kanji*.

OFFICIAL RECORDS

This illustrated scroll records the visit of Emperor Go-Mizunoo (who ruled from 1611–1629) to Shogun Tokugawa Iemitsu. The writing tells us that the palanquin (litter) in the picture carries the empress and gives a list of presents for the shogun.

Writing and Drawing

THE JAPANESE LANGUAGE belongs to a family of languages that includes Finnish, Turkish and Korean. It is totally different from its neighboring language, Chinese. Yet, for many centuries, Chinese characters were used for reading and writing Japanese. This was because people such as monks, courtiers and the emperor—the only people who could read and write—valued Chinese civilization and ideas.

As the Japanese kingdom grew stronger, and Japanese culture developed, it became clear that a new way of writing Japanese was required. Around A.D. 800, two new *kana* (ways of writing) were invented. Both used symbols developed from Chinese characters that expressed sounds and were written using a brush and ink on scrolls of paper. One type, called *hiragana*, was used for purely Japanese words; the other, called *katakana*, was used for words from elsewhere.

CALLIGRAPHY

You will need: paper, ink, a calligraphy brush. (You can use an ordinary paint brush and black paint if you cannot find a calligraphy brush or any ink.)

The numbers show the order of the strokes required for this character. Strokes 2, 3 & 4, and 5 & 6 are written in one movement, without lifting the brush.

1 The first stroke is called *soku*. Begin near the top of the paper, going from left to right. Move the brush sharply toward the bottom left, then lift it off the paper.

2 Strokes 2, 3 and 4 are called *roku*, *do* and *yaku*. Write them together in one movement. Apply pressure as you begin each stroke and then release again.

44

STORIES ON SCROLLS

Scrolls such as this one were designed to be hand-held, like a book. Words and pictures are side-by-side. Japanese artists often painted buildings with the roofs off, so that readers could see inside.

PAINTING PICTURES

A young boy is shown here mixing ink for his female companion. The ink is made from compressed charcoal that is dissolved in water to give the ink the required consistency. The artist herself has selected a broad brush to begin her painting.

PRINTED PICTURES

Woodblock pictures were created by carving an image in reverse on a block of wood, then using the block to print many copies of the same scene. Several different woodblocks might be used to print a single picture, one separate for each color.

3 For stroke 5 (*saku*), apply an even amount of pressure as you draw your brush left to right. For 6 (*ryo*), apply pressure at the beginning and release it.

4 Stroke 7 is called *taku*. Apply even pressure overall to make this short stroke. Make sure that you also make the stroke quite quickly.

5 Stroke 8 is also called *taku*. Apply an increasing amount of pressure as the brush travels down. Turn the brush back to the right at the last moment, as shown.

This character is called EI (eternal). It uses all eight major Japanese calligraphy strokes.

Poems, Letters and Novels

NEW WAYS OF WRITING the Japanese language were invented around A.D. 800. This led to the growth of forms of literature such as diaries, travel writing and poems. Elegant, refined poetry (called *waka*) was very popular at the emperor's court. From about 1600, *haiku* (short poems with 17 syllables) became the favorite form. *Haiku* were written by people from the samurai class, as well as by courtiers.

Women prose writers were especially important in early Japan. The courtier Sei Shonagon (born around A.D. 965) won praise for her *Pillow Book*—a kind of diary. Women writers were so famous that at least one man pretended to be a woman. The male poet Ki no Tsurayuki wrote *The Tosa Diary* under a woman's name.

LITERARY LADY
Lady Chiyo was a courtier and poet in the 1700s. Nobles read and wrote a lot of poetry. It was considered a sign of good breeding to quote from literary works. Letters to and from nobles often contained lines from poems.

THE WORLD'S FIRST NOVEL
This scroll shows a scene from the *Tale of Genji*, written in about A.D. 1000 by Lady Murasaki Shikibu. The scroll was painted in the 1700s, but the artist has used a painting style from the period in which the story was written.

MAKE PAPER

You will need: 8 pieces of wood (4 13 in and 4 11 in), nails, hammer, muslin (14 x 12 in), staple gun, electrical tape, scissors, torn-up paper, water bowl, potato masher, bowl, flower petals, spoon, soft cloths.

1 Ask an adult to make two frames. Staple stretched muslin onto one frame. Cover the frame with electrical tape to make the screen, as shown.

2 Put the frame and screen to one side. Soak paper scraps overnight in water. Mash into a pulp with the potato masher. It should look like oatmeal.

3 Half-fill the bowl with the pulp and cold water. You can add a few flower petals for decoration. Mix well with a spoon.

JAPANESE PAPER

Japanese craftworkers made many different kinds of beautiful paper. They used tree bark (especially the bark of the mulberry tree) or other plant fibers, which they blended carefully to create different thicknesses and textures of paper. They sometimes sprinkled the paper mixture with mica or gold leaf to produce rich, sparkling effects.

Japanese paper

mulberry bark

CRANES ON A CARD

This poem-card contains a traditional *waka* (palace-style) poem, in 31 syllables. It is written in silver and black and decorated with cranes.

POET AND TRAVELLER

The poet Matsuo Basho (1644-1694) is portrayed in this print dating from the 1800s. Basho was famous as a writer of *haiku* poems. He was also a great traveler, and in this picture he is shown (*right*) talking to two farmers he has met on his travels. Here is a typical example of a *haiku* by Basho:

> *The summer grasses—*
> *All that has survived from*
> *Brave warriors' dreams.*

The personality of a Japanese writer was judged by the type of paper they used, as well as by the content of the letter.

4 Place the screen with the frame on top into the bowl. As the frame and screen enter the water, scoop under the pulpy mixture.

5 Pull the screen out of the pulp, keeping it level. Gently move it from side to side over the bowl to let a layer of pulp form. Shake the water off.

6 Take the frame off the screen. Carefully lay the screen face down on a cloth. Mop the back of the screen with a cloth to get rid of the excess water.

7 Peel off the screen. Let the paper dry for at least 6 hours. When dry, turn over and gently peel off the cloth to reveal your paper.

At the Theater

GOING TO THE THEATER and listening to music were popular pastimes in ancient Japan. There were several kinds of Japanese drama. They developed from religious dances at temples and shrines, or from slow, stately dances performed at the emperor's court.

Noh is the oldest form of Japanese drama. It developed in the 1300s from rituals and dances that had been performed for centuries before. Noh plays were serious and dignified. The actors performed on a bare stage, with only a backdrop. They chanted or sang their words, accompanied by drums and a flute. Noh performances were traditionally held in the open air, often at a shrine.

Kabuki plays were first seen around 1600. In 1629, the shoguns banned women performers, so male actors took their places. Kabuki plays became very popular in the new, fast-growing towns.

GRACEFUL PLAYER
This woman entertainer is holding a *shamisen*—a three-stringed instrument, played by plucking the strings. The *shamisen* often formed part of a group, together with a *koto* (zither) and flute.

POPULAR PUPPETS
Bunraku (puppet plays) originated about 400 years ago, when *shamisen* music, dramatic chanting and hand-held puppets were combined. The puppets were so large and complex that it took three men to move them around on stage.

NOH THEATER MASK

You will need: tape measure, balloon, newspaper, bowl, glue, petroleum jelly, pins, scissors, felt-tip pen, modeling clay, awl, paints (red, yellow, black, and white), paintbrush, water container, cord.

1 Ask a friend to measure around your head above the ears. Blow up a balloon to match this measurement. This will be the base for the papier-mâché.

2 Rip up strips of newspaper. Soak in a water and glue mixture (1 part glue to 2 parts water). Cover the balloon with a layer of petroleum jelly.

3 Cover the front and sides of your balloon with a layer of papier-mâché. Let dry. Repeat 2 or 3 times. When dry, pop the balloon.

TRAGIC THEATER

An audience watches a scene from an outdoor performance of a Noh play. Noh drama was always about important and serious topics. Favorite subjects were death and the afterlife, and the plays were often very tragic.

LOUD AND FAST

Kabuki plays were a complete contrast to Noh. They were fast-moving, loud, flashy and very dramatic. Audiences admired the skills of the actors as much as the cleverness or thoughtfulness of the plots.

BEHIND THE MASK

This Noh mask represents a warrior's face. Noh drama did not try to be lifelike. The actors all wore masks and moved very slowly, using stiff, stylized gestures to express their feelings. Noh plays were all performed by men. Actors playing women's parts wore female clothes and masks.

Put on your mask and try to feel like an actor in an ancient Noh play. Imagine that you are wearing his long, swirling robes, too.

4 Trim the papier-mâché so that it forms a mask shape. Ask a friend to mark where your eyes, nose and mouth are when you hold it to your face.

5 Cut out the face holes with scissors. Put clay beneath the side of the mask at eye level. Use an awl to make two holes on each side.

6 Paint the face of a young lady on your mask. Use this picture as your guide. The mask would have been worn by a man.

7 Run the cord through the holes at each side. Tie one end. Once you have adjusted the mask so that it fits, tie the other end.

Travel and Transport

JAPAN IS A RUGGED and mountainous country. Until the twentieth century, the only way to travel through its wild countryside was along narrow, zig-zagging paths. These mountain paths and fragile wooden bridges across deep gullies and rushing streams were often swept away by landslides or floods.

During the Heian period, wealthy warriors rode fine horses, while important officials, wealthy women, children and priests traveled in lightweight wood and bamboo carts. These carts had screens and curtains for privacy and were pulled by oxen. In places where the route was unsuitable for ox-carts, wealthy people were carried shoulder-high on palanquins (lightweight portable boxes or litters). Ordinary people mostly traveled on foot.

During the Tokugawa period (1600–1868), the shoguns encouraged new road building as a way of increasing trade and control. The longest road was the Eastern Sea Road, which ran for 288 miles between Kyoto and the shogun's capital, Edo. Some people said it was the busiest road in the world.

BEASTS OF BURDEN
A weary mother rests with her child and ox during their journey. You can see that the ox is loaded up with heavy bundles. Ordinary people could not afford horses, so they used oxen to carry heavy loads or to pull carts.

SHOULDER HIGH
Noblewomen on palanquins (litters) are shown being taken by porters across a deep river. Some of the women have decided to disembark so they can be carried across the river. Palanquins were used in Japan right up to the Tokugawa period (1600–1868). When making journeys to or from the city of Edo, daimyo and wives were sometimes carried the whole route in palanquins.

HUGGING THE COASTLINE

Ships sail into harbor at Tempozan, Osaka. Cargo between Edo and Osaka was mostly carried by ships that hugged the coastline. The marks on the sails show the company that owned the ships.

CARRYING CARGO

Little cargo-boats, such as these at Edobashi in Edo, carried goods along rivers or around the coast. They were driven through the water by men rowing with oars or pushing against the river bed with a long pole.

STEEP MOUNTAIN PATHS

Travelers on mountain paths hoped to find shelter for the night in villages, temples or monasteries. It could take all day to walk 10 miles along rough mountain tracks.

IN THE HARBOR

Sea-going sailing ships, laden with cargo, are shown here at anchor in the harbor of Osaka (an important port in south-central Japan). In front of them you can see smaller riverboats with tall sails. Some families both lived and worked on riverboats.

Remote from the World

JAPAN'S GEOGRAPHICAL POSITION has always kept it separate from the rest of the world, but this has not meant total isolation. The Japanese have established links with their nearest neighbors and, sometimes, with lands far away.

In A.D. 588, the first Buddhist temple was built in Japan. Its construction marked the beginning of an era when Chinese religious beliefs, styles in art, clothes and painting, and beliefs about government and society began to play an important part in Japan. This Chinese-style era ended between A.D. 800 and 900. By that time, Japanese culture had grown strong and confident.

The next important contact with foreigners came when European traders and missionaries arrived in Japan in the 1540s. At first they were tolerated but, between 1635 and 1640, the shoguns banned Christianity altogether and strictly limited the places where foreigners could trade. Europeans had to live within the Dutch trading factory (trading post) on Dejima Island. Chinese merchants were allowed in only a few streets in Nagasaki. This policy of isolationism continued until 1853, when the United States sent gunboats and demands to trade. Reluctantly, the Japanese agreed and, in 1858, they signed a treaty of friendship with America.

KONG FUZI
The Chinese thinker and teacher Kong Fuzi (often known as Confucius) lived from 551 to 479 B.C. His ideas about family life, government and society influenced many later generations in both China and Korea. Chinese scribes took Kong Fuzi's ideas to Japan in about A.D. 552.

IN WESTERN STYLE
The young Emperor Meiji took over from the shoguns in 1868. In this picture, leading members of his government meet to discuss foreign policy in 1877. Most of them are wearing Western-style army and navy uniforms.

BLACK SHIPS

The terrifying Black Ships sailed into Japanese waters in 1853 and 1854. They were members of the United States Navy's squadron of steam-powered paddle-ships under the command of Matthew Perry. Commander Perry's orders were to demand Japanese cooperation with American plans for international trade. Faced with the threat of gunfire, the Japanese government eventually agreed.

GARDENING AT DEJIMA

The land around this house on Dejima Island has been made into a small garden. This island in Nagasaki harbor was the only area where Europeans were allowed to stay during Japan's period of isolation from the world.

BUSINESS IN DEJIMA

This painting from the 1700s portrays European and Japanese merchants and their servants at the Dutch trading factory at Dejima. The artist has shown the merchants discussing business and having tea in a Japanese-style house furnished with some European-style contents.

IDEAS FROM ABROAD

An American-style steam train travels across Yokohama harbor. This print is from the Meiji era (1868 onward), the period when Western ideas were introduced by the emperor. In the background you can see Yokohama docks which became a major center of new industries in the late 1800s.

Gods and Spirits

ALMOST ALL OF THE Japanese people followed a very ancient religious faith called Shinto. Shinto means the way of the gods. It developed from a central idea that all natural things had a spiritual side. These natural spirits—called *kami* in Japanese—were often kindly, but could be powerful or even dangerous. They needed to be respected and worshipped. Shinto also encouraged ancestor-worship—ancestor spirits could guide, help and warn. Special priests, called shamans, made contact with all these spirits by chanting, fasting or by falling into a trance.

Shinto spirits were honored at shrines that were often built close to sites of beauty or power, such as waterfalls or volcanoes. Priests guarded the purity of each shrine, and held rituals to make offerings to the spirits. Each Shinto shrine was entered through a *torii* (gateway), which marked the start of the sacred space. *Torii* always had the same design, based on the ancient perches of birds waiting to be sacrificed.

AT THE SHRINE
A priest worships by striking a drum at the Grand Shrine at Izu, one of the oldest Shinto shrines in Japan. A festival is held there every August, with processions, offerings and prayers. An *omikoshi* (portable shrine) is carried through the streets, so that the spirits can bring blessings to everyone.

OFFERINGS TO THE SPIRITS
Worshippers at Shinto shrines leave offerings for the *kami* (spirits) that live there. These offerings are neatly-wrapped barrels of *sake* (rice wine). Today, worshippers also leave little wooden plaques with prayers on them.

VOTIVE DOLLS

You will need: self-drying clay, 2 balsa wood sticks (5 in long), ruler, paints, paintbrush, water container, modeling clay, silver foil, red paper, gold paper, scissors, pencil, glue stick, optional basket and dowel.

1 Place a ball of clay on the end of each of the balsa sticks. On one of the sticks, push the clay down so that it is ¼ in from the end. This will be the man.

2 Paint hair and features on the man. Stand it up in modeling clay to dry. Repeat with the woman. Cover the ¼ in excess stick on the man's head in foil.

3 Take two pieces of red paper, 2½ x 5½ in and 2½ x 4 in. Fold them in half. Take two pieces of gold paper, 4½ x 4 in and ½ x 3 in. Fold in half.

HOLY VOLCANO

Fuji-San (Mount Fuji) has been honored as a holy place since the first people arrived in Japan. Until 1867, women were not allowed to set foot on Fuji's holy ground.

LUCKY GOD

Daikoku is one of seven lucky gods from India, China and Japan that are associated with good fortune. In Japan, he is the special god of farmers, wealth, and of the kitchen. Daikoku is recognized by both Shinto and Buddhist religions.

FLOATING GATE

This *torii* at Miyajima (Island of Shrines), in southern Japan, is built on the seashore. It appears to float on the water as the tide flows in. Miyajima was sacred to the three daughters of the sun.

In some regions of Japan, little dolls like these are put on display every year at Hinamatsuri (Girl's Day) on March 3rd.

4 Take the folded red paper (2½ x 5½ in). This is the man's *kimono*. Cut a triangular shape out of the bottom. Cut a neck hole out at the folded end.

5 Dip the blunt end of the pencil in white paint. Stipple a pattern on the red paper. Add the central dots using the pencil tip dipped in paint.

6 Slip the man's head and body into the red paper *kimono*. Then take the larger piece of gold paper and fold around the stick, as shown. Glue in place.

7 Now stick the gold paper (½ x 3 in) onto the woman's *kimono*, in the middle. Slip the woman's head and body into the *kimono*. Glue in place.

Monks and Priests

As well as following Shinto, many Japanese people also practiced the Buddhist faith. Prince Siddhartha Gautama, the founder of Buddhism, was born in Nepal around 500 B.C. He left his home to teach a new religion based on the search for truth and harmony and the ending of all selfish desires. His followers called him the Buddha (the enlightened one). The most devoted Buddhists spend at least part of their life as scholars, priests, monks or nuns.

Buddhist teachings first reached Japan in A.D. 552, brought by monks and scribes from China and Korea. Buddhism encouraged learning and scholarship and, over the centuries, many different interpretations of the Buddha's teachings developed. Each was taught by dedicated monks or priests and attracted many followers. The Buddhist monk Shinran (1173–1262) urged his followers to place their faith in Amida Buddha (a calm, kindly form of the Buddha). He taught them that Amida Buddha would lead them after death to the Western Paradise. Shinran's rival, Nichiren (1222–1282), claimed that he had been divinely chosen to spread the True Word. This was Nichiren's own interpretation of Buddhism, based on an ancient Buddhist text called the *Lotus Sutra*.

MONK AND PUPIL
A Buddhist sage is pictured with one of his pupils. Thanks to such teachers, Buddhist ideas spread beyond the imperial court to reach ordinary people, and many Buddhist temples and monasteries were built.

FAMOUS MONK
This woodcut from 1857 shows an episode from a story about the Buddhist monk, Nichiren. He was said to have calmed a storm by the power of his prayers. The influence of Nichiren continued long after his death, and many other stories were told about him.

SCHOLAR MONKS

A group of monks (*left*) study Buddhist scrolls. Monks were among the most important scholars in early Japan. They studied ancient Chinese knowledge and developed new Japanese ideas.

GREAT BUDDHA

This huge bronze statue of Daibutsu (the Great Buddha) is 37 feet high and weighs 93 tons. It was made at Kamakura in 1252—a time when the city was rich and powerful. The statue shows the Buddha in Amida form—inviting worshippers to the Western Paradise.

GOD OF MERCY

Standing over 16 feet high, this statue of Kannon was made around A.D. 700. Kannon is also known as the god of mercy. Originally, Kannon was a man— in fact, one form of the Buddha himself. However, over the years it became the custom to portray him in a female shape.

HOLY FLOWERS

The lotus flower often grows in dirty water and was believed to symbolize the purity of a holy life. It has many associations in literature with Buddhism. Chrysanthemums are often placed on graves or on Buddhist altars in the home. White and yellow flowers are most popular because these colors are associated with death.

white chrysanthemum

yellow chrysanthemums

lotus

HOLY WORDS

For many years after Buddhism reached Japan, it was practiced mainly by educated, wealthy people. Only they could read the beautiful Buddhist *sutras* (religious texts) like this one, created between A.D. 645 and 794. This sutra was written by hand, but some of the world's first printed documents are Buddhist *sutras* made in Japan.

Temples and Gardens

Land suitable for growing plants was very precious in Japan, so the people made the best use of it—both for growing food and for giving pleasure. All Japanese people who could afford it liked to surround their homes with beautiful gardens where they could enjoy gentle exercise, read or entertain.

Japanese gardens were often small, but they were carefully planned to create a landscape in miniature. Each rock, pool, temple and gateway was positioned where it could best be admired, but also where it formed part of a balanced, harmonious arrangement. Japanese designers chose plants to create a garden that would look good during all the different seasons of the year. Zen gardens—made of stones, sand and gravel—contained no plants at all.

PLANTS TO ADMIRE
Artists created and recorded delicate arrangements of blooms and leaves. This scroll-painting of branches, blossom and flowers dates from the 1500s.

ZEN GARDEN
This is part of a Zen Buddhist garden, made of lumps of rock and carefully-raked gravel. Gardens like this were designed to help people pray and meditate in peaceful surroundings.

HARMONY IN DESIGN
The Eastern Pagoda at the Yakushiji Temple in Nara is one of the oldest temples in Japan. It was founded in A.D. 680 and the pagoda was built in 730. Pagodas are tall towers, housing statues of Buddha or other religious works of art. Often, they form part of a group of buildings standing in a garden.

MAKING AN *IKEBANA* ARRANGEMENT
You will need: vase filled with water, scissors, twig, raffia or string, 2 flowers (with different length stems), a branch of foliage, 2 stems of waxy leaves.

1 Cut the twig so that it can be wedged into the neck of the vase. This will provide a structure to build on and to control the position of the flowers.

2 Remove the twig from the vase. Next, using raffia or string, tie the twig tightly onto the longest flower about halfway down the stem.

3 Place the flower stem in the vase. As you do this, gently slide the twig back into the neck of the vase and wedge it into position as before.

Trees in Miniature

Bonsai is the Japanese art of producing miniature but fully-formed trees. This is achieved by clipping roots and carefully regulating the water supply. Bonsai originated in China, but became popular in Japan around 1500. A tree that might naturally grow to about 18 feet could end up just 12 inches tall after bonsai treatment. Some bonsai trees are grown to achieve a dramatic slanting or twisted shape.

bonsai maple   *bonsai pine*

Gardeners at Work

A gardener, his wife and son prepare to plant cedar tree saplings. In the foreground, you can see a wooden bucket for watering plants, and a wooden hoe for digging up weeds. At the back, there are nursery beds, where seedlings are carefully tended. Cedar trees were, and still are, popular in Japan. The wood is used in the building of houses, and the beautiful trees themselves are used to decorate many gardens.

Chinese Style

The Tenryuji Temple, Kyoto, stands in one of the oldest Buddhist gardens still surviving in Japan. The garden was created before 1300. It is designed in the Chinese style and made of rocks, gravel, water and evergreen plants.

Ikebana means "living flowers." The three main branches of an arrangement represent heaven, earth and humans.

4 Add the shorter-stemmed flower to the longer stem. Position it so that it slants forward. Carefully lean it against the twig and the longer stem.

5 Slip the branch of foliage between the two stems. It should lean out and forward. The foliage should look as though it is a branch growing naturally.

6 Position some waxy leaves at the neck of the vase. *Ikebana* is floral arrangement using balance and form. Foliage is as important as the flowers.

7 Add a longer stem of waxy leaves at the back of the vase. This simple arrangement is typical of those Japanese people have in their homes.

59

Festivals and Ceremonies

T HE JAPANESE PEOPLE CELEBRATED FESTIVALS (*matsuri*) all year round, but especially during the warm months of spring and summer. Many of these festivals had ancient origins and were connected with farming or to the seasons. Others were linked to Shinto beliefs or to imported Buddhist ideas. There were two main kinds of festival. National holidays, such as New Year, were celebrated throughout Japan. Smaller local festivals were often linked to a Buddhist statue or temple, or to an ancient Shinto shrine.

One of the most important ceremonies was the tea ceremony, first held by Buddhist monks between 1300 and 1500. During the ceremony, the host served tea to his or her guests with great delicacy, politeness and precision.

BOWLS FOR TEA
At a tea ceremony, two types of green tea are served in bowls like these. The bowls are often plainly shaped and simply decorated. According to Zen beliefs, beauty can be found in pure, calm, simple things. Toyotomi Hideyoshi fell out with the tea master Sen no Rikyu over this. Hideyoshi liked tea bowls to be ornate rather than plain.

LOCAL FESTIVAL
A crowd of people enjoy a festival day. Local festivals usually included processions of portable Shinto shrines through the streets. These were followed by lots of noisy and cheerful people.

TEA BOWL

You will need: self-drying clay, cutting board, ruler, modeling tool, cut-out bottom of a plastic bottle (about 4in in diameter), fine sandpaper, paints, paintbrush, water container, soft cloth, varnish and brush.

1 Roll out a snake of clay 10 in long and ¹/₂ in thick. Starting from the center, curl the clay tightly into a circle with a diameter of 4 in.

2 Once you have made the base of the bowl, start to build up the sides. Roll out more snakes of clay, 10 in long. Join the pieces by pressing them together.

3 Sculpt the ridges of the coil bowl together using your fingers and the modeling tool. Use the bottom of a plastic bottle for support (See step 4).

CHERRY BLOSSOM

This woodblock print shows two women dressed in their best *kimonos* strolling along an avenue of flowering cherry trees. The cherry-blossom festival, called Hanami, was a time to meet friends and enjoy an open-air meal in the spring sunshine. Blossoms appeared in late February in the far south, but not until early May in the colder northern lands of Japan.

BLOSSOM

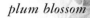

The Japanese looked forward to the sight of plum blossoms emerging, usually in mid February. The plum tree was the first to blossom. In March and April, cherry trees followed suit by producing clouds of delicate pink and white blossoms. People hurried to admire the cherry blossoms before their fragile beauty faded away. This joyful festival was also tinged with sadness. One storm could cause the blossom to fail. The cherry trees were a reminder that human lives, like blossoms, are very fragile.

plum blossom

cherry blossom

TEA CEREMONY

Hostess and guests sit politely on *tatami* (straw mats) for a Zen tea ceremony. This ritual often lasted for up to four hours. Many people in Japan still hold tea ceremonies, as a way of maintaining a revered social custom.

Design your bowl in a pure, elegant style, like the Zen potters. If you want to add any decoration, make sure it is very simple, too.

4 Roll out another coil of clay 7½ in long and ½ in wide. Make it into a circle 3 in in diameter. Join the ends. This will form a stand for the bowl.

5 Turn the bowl over— still using your soda bottle for support. Join the circular stand to the bottom of the bowl. Mold it on using your fingers.

6 Let the bowl dry. Once dry, remove the plastic bottle and sand the bowl gently. Paint the base color over it. Set aside until dry.

7 Apply your second color using a cloth. Lightly dapple paint over the bowl to make it appear like a glaze. Varnish the bowl inside and out.

Glossary

A

Ainu The original inhabitants of northern Japan.

akido A Japanese martial art in which players try to overbalance their opponents.

ancestor A family member who died long ago.

ashigaru A samurai (warrior) with a low rank.

B

barter The exchange of goods for others of equal value.

Buddha The name (meaning "the enlightened one") given to Siddhartha Gautama, an Indian prince who lived around 500 B.C. He taught a new philosophy, based on seeking peace (*nirvana*).

Buddhism A world faith, based on the Buddha's teachings.

bugaku An ancient dance form that was popular at the court of the Japanese emperor.

bunraku Japanese puppet plays.

bushido A strict code of brave, honorable behavior, meant to be followed by samurai (warriors).

C

clan A group of people related to each other by ancestry or marriage.

D

daimyo A nobleman or warlord.

dynasty The successive generations of a ruling family.

G

garrison A fort or similar place that is guarded by a troop of soldiers. The word garrison can also refer to the troop of soldiers.

geta Wooden clogs, designed to keep feet dry in wet weather.

guilds Groups of skilled workers who checked quality standards, trained young people and looked after old and sick members.

H

haiku A short poem containing 17 syllables. Haiku were popular after about A.D. 1600.

Haniwa Clay figures that were buried in ancient Japanese tombs. They are a very important source of evidence about early Japan.

I

ikat A weaving technique. The threads are dyed in many different colors then woven together to create complicated and beautiful patterns.

ikebana The art of flower-arranging that is practiced in Japan.

inro A small decorated box, worn hung from the belt. Originally, *inro* were designed for storing medicines.

inscribed Something that is carved on stone or another hard material.

J

Jomon An early hunter-gatherer civilization in Japan. It originated in about 10,000 B.C.

K

kabuki Popular plays, performed in Japan from about A.D. 1600. They were fast-moving and loud.

kami The Japanese holy spirits.

kana The name for the Japanese method of writing.

kanji The picture-symbols that were used for writing Japanese before about A.D. 800.

kendo A martial art in which players fight one another with bamboo swords.

kimono A loose robe with wide sleeves, worn by both men and women.

kuzu A plant with a fleshy root that is dried and used in traditional medicine.

L

lacquer A shiny varnish made from the sap of trees.

litter A portable bed.

loom A piece of equipment used to weave cloth.

M

mausoleum A burial chamber.

mica A flaky, shiny mineral.

millet A grass-like plant that produces edible seeds.

monsoon Winds that blow at particular seasons of the year in south Asia, bringing heavy rain.

mosaics Tiny pieces of colorful stone, shell or glass that are used to make pictures or to decorate objects.

mother-of-pearl The beautiful shiny coating that forms on the inside of an oyster shell.

N

nape The back of the neck.

netsuke Small toggles, carved from ivory and used to attach items to belts.

noh A serious, dignified drama that originated in Japan around A.D. 1300.

O

obi A wide sash worn only by women.

omikashi A portable shrine.

P

pagoda A tall tower, usually part of a Buddhist temple.

peninsula An area of land surrounded by water on three sides, making it almost like an island.

pillow book A collection of short notes and writings, rather like a diary.

plate-armor Protective clothing made of overlapping plates of metal.

R

ramie A plant like flax, used to make clothing.

regent Someone who rules a country on behalf of another person.

S

sake Rice wine.

shamisen A three-stringed musical instrument.

samurai Well-trained warriors.

scroll-painting A painting on a long roll of paper.

shinden A large, single-story house in Japan.

shinto An ancient Japanese religion, known as the "way of the gods", based on honoring holy spirits.

shrine A holy place used for Shinto worship.

shoen A private estate in the country.

shogun A Japanese army commander. From 1185-1868, shoguns ruled Japan.

silken Made of silk.

sumo A type of wrestling popular in Japan.

surcoat A long, loose tunic worn over armor.

T

tachi The long sword that was carried by a samurai.

tanbo Flooded fields where rice is grown.

tatami A mat woven from reeds that covers the floor.

tenshu The tall central tower of a castle.

terracotta Baked clay.

threshing Separating grains of wheat or rice from their stalks.

tofu Beancurd—a nourishing food made from the pulp of crushed soybeans.

torii The traditional gateway to a Shinto shrine.

U

uji A clan.

W

waka Elegant poetry, popular at the emperor's court.

winnowing Separating grains of wheat and rice from their papery outer layer called chaff.

Y

yoke A long piece of wood or bamboo used to help carry heavy loads. The yoke was placed across the shoulders and a load was hung from each end to balance it.

Z

Zen A branch of the Buddhist faith that was popular among the samurai.

Index

A
Ainu people 4, 7
Amida Buddha 56
armor 16-17

B
bonsai 59
bows and arrows 17, 18
Buddhism 5, 6, 8, 11,
    18-19, 42, 52, 56-8, 59,
    60-1
bugaku 12
bunraku 48
bushido 18

C
calligraphy 43-5
carp streamer 26-7
castles 5, 9, 15, 32-3, 34
children 26-7, 45
China 6, 7, 8, 52
climate 5, 38, 39
cloth and clothes 4, 17, 26,
    34-42
Confucius *see* Kong Fuzi
cosmetics 36
courtiers 12-13, 36-7, 46

D
daimyo 5, 8-9, 16-18, 32-3, 34
dance 34-5
Dejima Island 52-53
dolls 54-55

E
earthquakes 28
Edo 9, 50
emperors 4, 5, 6-9, 10-11,
    12, 13, 16

F
family life 26-7
fans 36-7
farming 4, 6, 8, 9, 11, 20-1,
    24, 26, 38-9
festivals 27, 60-1
fish and shellfish 4, 20, 22-3
flowers 57, 58-9, 61
food 20-5
foreigners, contact with 4, 7,
    8, 9, 52-3
Fuji, Mount 5, 7, 55
Fujiwara clan 6, 13

G
gardens 58-9
geishas 35
Gemmei, Empress 10, 30
geta 37
Godaigo, Emperor 8
Go-Mizunoo, Emperor 44

H
haiku 46-7
hairstyles 36-7, 38
Haniwa figures 10
Heian-kyo 6, 30-2
Heian period 6, 7, 50
Heiji civil war 7, 14
helmets 16-19, 40
Hideyoshi, Toyotomi 9, 32,
    60
Himeji Castle 9, 32
Hiroshige 43
Hokkaido 5, 6, 7
Honshu 5, 6, 7
housing 28-31

I
ikebana 58-9
inro 40-1
islands 5, 6-7, 22
Izu 54

J
Jingu, Empress 8
Jomon people 4, 6, 22

K
Kabuki theater 9, 48-9
Kamakura 7, 14
Kammu, Emperor 6, 30
kanji 34, 44-5
Kannon 57
Uesugi Kenshin 18
kimonos 26, 34, 36-7, 40,
    61
Ki no Tsurayuki 46
kites 14-15, 27
Kofun (Old Tomb) period 5
Kokiji 6
Komyo, Emperor 8
Kong Fuzi (Confucius) 7, 52
Korea 7
koto 29
Kotoku, Emperor 6
kuzu 27
Kyoto 6, 7, 14, 30-3, 34, 35,
    50, 59
Kyushu 5, 6, 7

L
lacquer 40-1
literature 7, 9, 46-7

M
martial arts 19
medicine 27
Meiji, Emperor 6, 9, 52, 53
metalwork 4, 5, 6, 16-17,
    40-1, 57
Minamoto Yoritomo 7, 14
Momoyama period 9
Mongols 6, 8
monks 51, 56-7
Murasaki Shikibu, Lady 7, 9,
    46
Muromachi period 8
music 29, 34-5, 48-9

N
Nara 6, 10, 11, 30, 58
netsuke 34, 40-1
Nijo Castle 15, 33
Nikko 15
Nintoku, Emperor 11
Nobunaga, Oda 9, 18, 33
Noh theater 48-9

O
obi 37
Okinawa Islands 7
onigiri 24-5
Onin War 8
origami 42-3

P
paddyfields 4, 20, 38
pagodas 58
painting 13, 14, 15, 17, 19,
    22, 42, 45, 58
palanquins 44, 50
paper 28, 29, 35, 36-7, 40,
    42-3, 46-7
parasols 35, 36
Perry, Commander Matthew
    9, 53
pottery 4, 6, 10, 25, 28, 35,
    40-1, 60-1
printing 7, 22, 29, 43, 45,
    56-7

R
religion 5, 6, 8, 10, 11, 18-
    19, 27, 42, 43, 54-7, 60
rice 4, 6, 7, 19, 20-1, 24-5,
    38

S
sake 21, 25, 54
samurai 4, 5, 7, 8, 9, 16-19,
    20, 25, 34, 35, 36, 40
screens 28-9, 33, 42
Sei Shonagon 7, 46
Shikoku 5, 6, 7
shinden 30-1
Shinto 43, 54-5, 60
shoguns 4, 6, 7, 9, 14-16,
    44, 50
Shotoku, Prince 11, 12
Shomu, Emperor 6, 11
silk 28, 35, 37
sumo wrestling 20
swords 8, 16, 18, 41

T
tachi 16
Taika Laws 12
Taira clan 7, 14
Tale of Genji, The 7, 9, 46
tea 25, 60-1
temples and shrines 10, 11,
    27, 30-1, 42, 51, 54-5, 58-9
theater 9, 34, 48-9
Tokugawa Ieyasu 6, 9, 15,
    32, 33, 44
Tokugawa period 8, 9, 15,
    16-17, 20, 50
Tokyo 9, 43
tombs 5, 10, 11, 15
torrii 7, 54-5
towns 34-5
trade 6, 7, 8, 9, 34-5, 39,
    51-3
transport 44, 50

V
volcanoes 4, 54-5

W
waka 46-7
women 7, 26-7, 35, 36-9,
    46, 55
woodworking 11, 28-9, 30-
    2, 34, 42-3, 59
writing 5, 6, 7, 34, 43-7

Y
Yamato period 5, 6, 10-11
Yayoi period 4

Z
Zen Buddhism 8, 18-19, 59,
    60-1